This copy of

THE GOOD EGG
YOLK BOOK

belongs to

_____

Also available in Beaver by Katie Wales

The Elephant Joke Book
The Return of the Elephant Joke Book
Jokes from Outer Space
Santa's Christmas Joke Book

THE GOOD EGG YOLK BOOK

Katie Wales

Illustrated by Mark Burgess

BEAVER BOOKS

To Tim – eggain!

A Beaver Book
Published by Arrow Books Limited
62–65 Chandos Place, London WC2N 4NW

An imprint of Century Hutchinson Ltd

London Melbourne Sydney Auckland
Johannesburg and agencies throughout the world

First published 1990

Set in Century Schoolbook
by JH Graphics Ltd, Reading

Made and printed in Great Britain
by Courier International Ltd
Tiptree, Essex

ISBN 0 09 965960 3

Contents

Good Egg Jokes

What is made of chocolate and is found on the sea-bed?
An oyster egg.

What happens to people who eat too many Easter eggs?
They take up two seats.

Where do blue Easter eggs come from?
Sad chickens.

'Where did you get that Easter tie?'
'Why do you call it that?'
'Well it's got egg all over it.'

Have you heard the joke about the three eggs?
Two bad!

'Doctor, doctor, my wife thinks she's a chicken.'
'Well, bring her to see me.'
'I can't, we can't do without the eggs!'

Knock, knock.
Who's there?
Egbert.
Egbert who?
Egbert no bacon.

Knock, knock.
Who's there?
Eggs.
Eggs who?
Eggstremely nice to meet you.

Knock, knock.
Who's there?
Four eggs.
Four eggs who?
Four eggsample.

What goes up brown and white and comes
down yellow and white?
An egg.

What's a Hindu?
Lay eggs.

What's another name for a mischievous egg?
A practical yolker.

Where do tough chickens come from?
Hard-boiled eggs.

Where does an egg come from if it is seen
floating down the Thames?
A chicken.

'Waiter, waiter, this egg is bad!'
'Don't blame me, sir, I only laid the table.'

How does a chick fit into an egg?
Eggs-actly.

Why does a hen lay eggs?
If she dropped them, they would break.

Why is a horse like an egg?
They must be broken before using.

When is a horse like a bad egg?
When it's (s)addled.

Why is an egg like a brick?
They both have to be laid.

Why did the hens refuse to lay any more eggs?
They were tired of working for chicken feed.

What kind of chickens lay electric eggs?
Battery hens.

What do you get when a chicken drinks whisky?
Scotch eggs.

What is the best day for making eggs and bacon?
Friday.

What did one egg say to another in the monastery?
'Out of the frying-pan and into the friar.'

What did two boiled eggs say in the saucepan?
'Phew, isn't it hot in here!'
'Yes, but wait till you get out – they'll bash your head in!'

What did the egg say to the whisk?
'I know when I'm beaten!'

Why did the comedian tell jokes to eggs?
He wanted to crack them up.

Why did the egg go into the jungle?
It was an eggs-plorer.

Could you kill a monster by throwing eggs at him?
Yes — he'd be eggs-terminated!

What kind of motorbike can cook eggs?
A scrambler.

What did the hen say when she saw a scrambled egg?
'What a crazy mixed up kid!'

Why is a scrambled egg like the England cricket team?
Both get beaten.

What is gegs?
Scrambled eggs.

What sort of food do fighter pilots eat?
Scramble eggs.

Why are cooks cruel?
They beat eggs.

How do monsters like their eggs?
Terrifried.

What would you get if you crossed a chicken with an electric organ?
Hammond eggs.

What would you get if you crossed a chicken with a waitress?
Neatly laid eggs.

What would you get if you crossed a chicken with gunpowder?
An eggs-plosion.

What would you get if you crossed a chicken with a gooseberry?
A hen that lays green and hairy eggs.

What would you get if you crossed a chicken
with a dog?
Pooched eggs.

What would you get if you crossed a chicken
with a kangaroo?
Pouched eggs.

What would you get if you crossed an egg with
an elephant?
An omelette that never forgets.

What's the difference between an elephant and
an egg?
I don't know.
I'm not trying one of your omelettes!

What's the difference between an elephant and
an egg sandwich?
A sandwich doesn't weigh two tons.

What's smooth, oval and very rich?
An eggs-travaganza.

Who is the egg's favourite female singer?
Yolko Ono.

Why did the pirate put a chicken where he buried his treasure?
Because eggs marked the spot.

Did you hear about the farmer who gave his chickens sawdust to eat by mistake?
When the eggs hatched, five had wooden legs and the sixth was a woodpecker!

Every morning the farmer had eggs for breakfast. He didn't have any chickens, and he didn't buy eggs. Where did he get them?
From his ducks.

Why couldn't Humpty Dumpty be put together again?
Because he wasn't everything he was cracked up to be.

What happened to Humpty Dumpty after he had a great fall?
He was made into an egg sandwich for all the king's men.

Where did Humpty Dumpty put his hat?
Humpty dumped his hat on the wall.

What happened to Humpty Dumpty the Wally?
The wall fell on him.

What is yellow and white and travels at 125mph?
An inter-city train driver's egg sandwich.

What is yellow and white and travels at 2000mph?
A Concorde pilot's egg sandwich.

What is the best way to make an egg roll?
Push it down a hill.

Who was Snow White's brother?
Egg White. Get the yolk?

What do you get if you cross egg white and gunpowder?
A boom-meringue.

What do you call a monkey with a sweet tooth?
A meringue-utang.

What is white and fluffy and swings from one
cakeshop to another?
A meringue-utang.

What is white and fluffy, has whiskers and
floats?
A cata-meringue.

What kind of meringues come back to you?
Boomeringues.

Long-playing Omelette Jokes

What's soft and yellow and goes round and round at 33rpm?
A long-playing omelette.

'Waiter, waiter, will the omelette be long?'
'No sir, round.'

What is as tall as the Post Office Tower and contains 100,000 eggs?
A multi-storey omelette.

What's soft and yellow and goes 'putt, putt'?
An outboard omelette.

What's soft and yellow, and goes 'bzzzz'?
An electric omelette.

What's soft and yellow and flickers?
An omelette with a loose connection.

Why did the elephant paint the soles of his feet yellow?
So he could hide upside down in an omelette pan.

Have you ever seen one hiding in an omelette pan?
No?
Well, that shows what a good disguise it is!

What's soft and yellow and takes Disprin?
An omelette with a headache.

What's soft and yellow and goes 'tick, tock'?
A clockwork omelette.

What's soft and yellow and wears a mask?
The Lone Omelette.

What's soft and yellow and always points north?
A magnetic omelette.

What's soft and yellow and goes up and down?
An omelette in a lift.

What's soft and yellow and red all over?
An omelette holding its breath.

What's soft and yellow and jumps up and down?
An omelette at a football match.

What is grey on the inside and yellow on the outside?
An elephant disguised as an omelette.

What's huge, soft and yellow, and goes 'fe-fi-fo-fum'?
A giant omelette.

What is soft and yellow and shoots out of the pan at 100mph?
An E-type omelette.

What's soft and yellow and coughs?
An omelette with a bad chest.

What is big and yellow and has a blocked trunk?
An elephant fallen into an omelette pan.

What's soft and yellow and makes pit stops?
A racing omelette.

What's soft and yellow and wears sunglasses?
An omelette on holiday.

What is soft yellow and goes 'slam, slam'?
A two-door omelette.

What is yellow outside, grey inside, and has a fantastic memory?
An elephant omelette.

What's soft and yellow and comes at you from all sides?
Quadraphonic omelette.

What is soft and yellow and explodes on your plate?
A Kamikaze omelette.

What weighs 2 tons, is grey, and loves omelettes?
A Spanish elephant.

What's soft and yellow and hairy?
An omelette dropped on the carpet.

What's soft and yellow and good at sums?
An omelette with a calculator.

What is soft and yellow and climbs trees?
An omelette. (I lied about it climbing trees.)

What's big, soft and yellow, and lives in
Scotland?
The Loch Ness Omelette.

What is soft and yellow and dangerous?
A shark-infested omelette.

What else?
An omelette with a machine-gun.

What else?
A thundering herd of omelettes.

What's soft and yellow and goes along the seabed?
An omelette in a submarine.

What goes 'trip, trip, SPLAT!'?
An elephant tripping over an omelette pan.

What is soft and yellow and needs no ironing?
A drip-dry omelette.

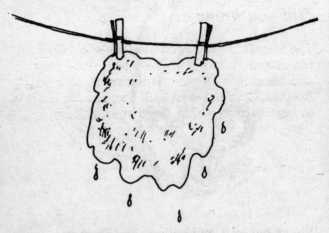

What is soft and yellow and can't sit down?
A seatless omelette.

What is soft and yellow and goes 'slam, slam'?
A two-door omelette.

It's EGGS-UBERANT! EGGS-ITING! –
EGGS-TRAVAGANT! EGGS-TRAORDINARY!
EGGS-ELLENT! EGGS-ENTRIC!
EGGS-EPTIONAL! EGGS-CLUSIVE!
EGGS-HILARATING! EGGS-PANSIVE!

Be an Eggspert:
Eggs-traordinary Facts

Did you know . . .

The largest bird's egg in the world is laid by
the ostrich. It can measure up to 20cm long
and 15cm in diameter: as big as 24 hens' eggs.
It takes 40 minutes to boil! The ostrich itself is
so big, its head would reach your ceiling!

Ostrich eggs were once thought to have magical powers. They were brought to England as strange objects by the Crusaders and early navigators. Many were decorated, or made into cups.

But some dinosaur eggs that have been found were bigger than ostrich eggs. Those of a type of lizard 80 million years ago were 30cm long. At present, it's the whale shark which holds the record for laying the biggest eggs in the world.

The smallest egg in the world is laid by the Jamaican hummingbird. It is less than 10mm long and weighs 3500 times less than an ostrich egg! Some hummingbirds are lighter than moths.

The largest egg laid by a British bird is the mute swan's: about 11–13cm long. The smallest British egg is the goldcrest's: 12–14mm long. The goldcrest itself is less than 9cm long.

There are more hens in Britain than there are people – and probably more than everyone in the world!

A chicken farm in Ohio has nearly 5 million hens, laying nearly 4 million eggs a day. Actually, if all the American eggs laid each year were put end to end they'd go round the world 100 times!

An average free range hen lays about 180 eggs a year. But a Black Orpington hen once laid 361 eggs in a year and a White Leghorn laid 371. Ducks, by the way, only lay eggs in the morning.

The highest number of yolks found in a chicken's egg is 9.

On average, we eat 250 eggs a year. But one man from Scotland once ate 38 soft-boiled eggs in 75 seconds!

The albatross's egg may take 80 days to hatch. And the baby bird waits 9 months before it leaves the nest! (A chick becomes a domestic hen in less than 2 months.) The albatross has a wing span as long as two tall men end to end.

It's the male emu and the male Emperor penguin which hatch the eggs. The penguin makes no nest: it holds the egg between its feet for more than 2 months, in temperatures as low as minus 60 degrees Celsius! Penguins also snore when they are asleep.

Owls don't build nests either. They lay eggs in holes usually or in other birds' old nests. And the 'fairy' tern just balances her egg on a bare branch! The ostrich lets the heat of the sun hatch its egg in the sand.

The cuckoo, of course, leaves its egg in occupied nests. The female cuckoo lays about 20 eggs this way each year. (The gannet may lay only one egg a year.)

Some wild birds' eggs are very valuable: rare hawks' eggs can fetch over £10,000 – but the trade in 'new' eggs is illegal because the theft of eggs from the nests of rare birds, like the red kite's in Wales, can endanger the species still further.

Some crocodiles' eggs have white yolks!

Fish eggs can also be very valuable – but for a different reason. The sturgeon's eggs (or roe) which we call caviar is the most expensive food in the world; 500 grammes cost well over £200. The passengers on the QE2 consume a third of the annual production of best caviar.

The termite can lay up to one egg per second! And it lives for 50 years!

Two blind men from Wiltshire shelled 1050 dozen hard-boiled eggs in just over 7 hours in 1971.

The longest egg and spoon race of nearly 46km was won in 4 hours 30 minutes in 1979.

How far can you throw a fresh egg without breaking it? Over 96m in Finland in 1981!

The biggest omelette in the world (54,763 eggs) was cooked in Las Vegas, Nevada in 1986. The largest pancake? 5274 eggs in Cheltenham in 1987. The largest Yorkshire pudding? 50 dozen eggs in 1986 in Bradford.

How long does it take to eat 62 pancakes?
Under 7 minutes is the record!

There's a kind of hen (the Araucana) which
lays ready-made Easter eggs! They're either
pink, purple, or green.

Talking of Easter eggs . . .

The Easter Eggs-perience

The heaviest Easter egg weighed 3430kg, and was made in Leicester in 1982. The tallest (5.78m) was made in Bedford in 1987.

The first chocolate Easter eggs were made 150 years ago, and were completely solid at first, not hollow. (Hollow eggs began in the 1920s.)

Before chocolate, Easter eggs to be eaten were made of marzipan or sugar; or were decorated hard-boiled eggs.

These decorated eggs were called 'Pasch', 'Pace', or 'Peace' eggs in different parts of the British Isles: from the French word *Pâques*, meaning Easter. Some people still dye hard-boiled eggs pretty colours by boiling them with onion skins and berries, etc; or they paint patterns or faces on the shells.

'Egg-hunting' is a traditional custom all over Europe. Decorated eggs are hidden in the garden on Easter Sunday. In Georgia in 1985, there took place the biggest egg-hunt in the world, involving 72,000 hard-boiled eggs, and 40,000 candy eggs. In France, children are told that they are brought by the Easter Bells; in Germany, that the Easter Hare leaves them in his Easter basket.

Indoors, in many countries in Europe, painted eggshells and tiny wooden rabbits are hung like Christmas tree decorations on branches of pussy willow and spring twigs.

Another old Easter custom is 'egg-rolling', where boiled eggs are rolled down slopes to see which ones roll the quickest or the farthest without damage. This is also a traditional custom in the grounds of the White House, the home of the US President. Started in the early years of the last century, 100,000 eggs are rolled there on Easter Monday – but plastic!

Eggs have been associated with Easter for hundreds of years. Early Christians used to take baskets of eggs to be blessed in Church on Easter Sunday. One belief is that the egg looks like the stone that covered the entrance to Christ's tomb, which was mysteriously moved.

From the beginning of Lent until Easter Sunday (40 days and nights), eating eggs used to be forbidden by the Christian Church. Lent is a time of fasting, or doing without food, so on the day before, Shrove Tuesday ('Confession' Tuesday), people used all their eggs up in pancakes. And we still have Pancake Day today! Then on Easter Sunday people would make huge omelettes – well, the chickens didn't know about Lent, and of course, they had just carried on laying eggs . . .

In Germany, there is a superstition that an egg laid on Good Friday will last for 100 years! Or, that if you eat an egg on Good Friday, it will keep you in good health.

But Easter eggs aren't only associated with Christianity. The word 'Easter' itself comes from a pagan Spring festival, to the goddess Eostre, associated with re-birth and fertility. (The Easter Hare mentioned above was supposed to be her companion.) The egg is a well-known symbol of fertility in ancient religions all over the world. So the ancient Egyptian priests, for example, refused to eat eggs; and in India, they used to believe that the world was made from a giant egg-shell, the two halves making the sky and earth. People in China gave each other red painted eggs at the Spring festival over 3000 years ago, and so too the Persians.

Easter eggs can also be carved in wood, marble, ivory, etc. Artificial Easter eggs were a popular fashion in the nineteenth century. The most expensive eggs of this kind are the famous Fabergé eggs exquisitely decorated with gold and precious stones and tiny secret compartments. Carl Fabergé was the court jeweller to the Russian Tsar, Alexander III, about 100 years ago.

Fowl Jokes . . .

Who tells fowl jokes?
Comedihens.

What's feathered, clucks, and a Wimbledon
champion?
Boris Pecker.

Why did the lady cover her ears when she
passed the chickens?
*Because she didn't want to hear their fowl
language.*

How do you make an elephant laugh?
Tell him a chicken joke.

Who is the better fighter: an elephant or a chicken?
An elephant — he's no chicken.

'Waiter, waiter, this chicken's a battery hen.'
'How can you tell, sir?'
'From the taste: it's shocking!'

Why did the chicken cross the road?
It's a fowl reason.

Why else?
To get to the other side.

Why else?
Because the subway was closed.

Why else?
To see a man lay bricks.

Why else?
It didn't want to hear that last joke.

Why else?
Because the light was green.

Why else?
To escape from Colonel Sanders.

Why else?
To prove it had guts.

Why did the chicken cross the road twice?
Because it was a double-crosser.

Why did the chicken only go half-way across the road?
Because she wanted to lay it on the line.

Why did the one-eyed chicken cross the road?
To go to the Birds Eye shop.

Why did the chicken cross the M25?
To commit suicide!

Why did the communist chicken cross the road?
It was a Rhode Island red.

Why did the fox cross the road?
Because the chicken was in its mouth.

Why did the hamster cross the road?
It was tied to the leg of a chicken.

Again — why did the chicken cross the road?
It was tied to the leg of an elephant.

Why did the elephant cross the road?
It was the chicken's day off.

Why else?
To pick up the squashed chicken.

Why did the elephant lie in the middle of the road?
To trip up chickens.

Why didn't the hen cross the road?
She chickened out.

Why else?
It was fowl on the other side.

Why did the chicken run on to the football pitch?
Because the referee had whistled for a fowl.

What would you get if you crossed a chicken with a guitar?
A chicken that makes music when you pluck it.

What would you get if you crossed a chicken with a cement-mixer?
A bricklayer.

What would you get if you crossed a chicken with a clock?
An alarm cluck.

What would you get if you crossed a chicken with a turkey?
A churkey.

What would you get if you crossed a chicken with a torch?
A battery hen.

What would you get if you crossed a chicken with a cow?
Roost beef.

What would you get if you crossed a chicken
with a waiter?
A hen that lays tables.

Can a dog make a rabbit hutch?
No, but a fox can make a chicken run.

What do foxes feel when they've eaten too
many chickens?
Down in the mouth.

What has feathers and purple feet?
A chicken that makes its own wine.

What do chickens drink?
Yolk-a-cola.

What goes 'cluck, cluck, bang!'?
A chicken in a mine-field.

What goes 'cluck, cluck, splash!'?
A chicken in a puddle.

What happened to the bad chicken?
She was eggs-ecuted.

What do chickens do at school?
Eggs-ams.

What happened to the chicken who ran away
from school?
She was eggs-pelled.

What does a chicken do in a science
laboratory?
Eggs-periments.

How do chickens like to travel?
With an eggs-cursion ticket.

What is a chicken's favourite pastime?
Eggs-ercise.

How do you make a chicken laugh?
Tell it an elephant joke.

Why do chickens go to the theatre?
For hentertainment.

Who is a chicken's favourite singer?
Egglebert Humperdink.

What is a chicken's favourite brand of petrol?
Shell.

What is a chicken's favourite type of car?
A hatch-back.

Why did the chicken run away from the farm?
She was tired of being cooped up.

Where do chickens like to live?
Hatch End.

Where else?
Eggbaston.

Where do chickens put their savings?
In the Eggs-chequer.

On which side does a chicken have the most feathers?
On the outside.

How do chickens start a race?
From scratch.

'Waiter, waiter, there's no chicken in this chicken pie.'
'So? You don't get a dog in a dog biscuit, do you?'

When is the best time to buy chickens?
When they're going cheap.

What do you call a greasy chicken?
A slick chick.

What bird runs away from a fight?
A chick, because it's yellow.

What did the chicks say to the shopkeeper?
'Cheap, cheap!'

What game do baby chicks play?
Peck-a-boo.

What did the chicken say to her chicks on their
first Easter?
'Don't get over eggs-cited.'

How do baby chickens dance?
Chick to chick.

Why does a chick walk softly?
Because it's a baby and can't walk hardly.

Did you hear about the baby chick who found
an orange in its nest, and said 'Look what
marmalade!'

Why was the chicken sick?
It had people pox.

What was the poor-sighted chicken doing in the
garden?
It was sitting on an egg-plant.

What happened when the Royal Navy fed
dynamite to hens?
It got mine layers.

Why is it a waste of time holding a party for chickens?
Because it's hard to make hens meet.

Why did the farmer put a computer in the hen-house?
To make the chickens multiply faster.

What did the Spanish farmer say to his chickens?
'Ole!'

What kind of cake should you serve to chickens?
Layer cake.

Name a famous building built by American chickens?
The Henpire State Building.

What's feathered, and crossed the Alps on elephants?
Hennibal's army.

Where does the Queen keep her chickens?
Royal Enfield.

Why don't elephants have feathers?
If they did, you'd confuse them with chickens.

What would happen if they did?
You'd be knee-deep in feathers!

What has two arms, two wings, two tails, three heads, and eight legs?
A man on a horse holding a chicken.

What's a ticklish subject?
The study of feathers.

What's watery, very frightened and full of feathers?
Chicken soup.

What has two legs, rides a broomstick, goes to the seaside, but won't go in the water?
A chicken sand-witch.

What did the cobbler say when six chickens came into his shop?
'Shoo!'

Why was the chicken sitting on an axe?
She was trying to hatchet.

Why did the cockerel cross the road?
For his own fowl purposes.

How do you stop a cockerel crowing on Monday morning?
Eat it for Sunday lunch.

Why did the cockerel refuse to fight?
Because he was chicken.

What's the opposite of cock-a-doodle-doo?
Cock-a-doodle-don't.

Why is a cockerel fussy?
Because he never lends his comb.

Why did the farmer call his cockerel Robinson?
Because it crew so.

Who takes longer to pack for his holiday, an elephant or a cockerel?
The elephant. He has to pack his trunk — the cockerel only has a comb.

Where do cockerels like to go for their holidays?
To London — there are lots of cockneys there.

What has feathers and goes 'C-c-c-c-c'?
A cockerel with a stammer.

What has feathers, and drives on French motorways?
Coq-au-van.

What would you get if you crossed a cockerel
with a giraffe?
An animal that wakes people on the top floor.

What would you get if you crossed a cockerel
with an elephant?
*An animal that wakes people living in the next
town.*

What would you get if you crossed a cockerel
with a chef?
A cook-a-doodle-doo.

What would you get if you crossed a cockerel
with a spaniel and a poodle?
A cocker-poodle-doo.

What does a ghost cockerel say?
'Spook-a-doodle-doo.'

Did you hear about the cockerel who fell in
love with a hen at first sight?
She egged him on a bit.

What's a goblet?
A small turkey.

What did the mother turkey say to her naughty
child?
*'If your father could see you now, he'd turn in
his gravy.'*

Where do good turkeys go when they die?
To oven.

Why did they let the turkey join the band?
Because he had drumsticks.

Why did the farmer cross a turkey with an octopus?
So his family could all have a leg each at Easter.

What unlocks a Turkish house?
A turkey.

Why do turkeys eat so little?
They're always stuffed.

What's the definition of a real goose?
Propaganda.

Did you ever see a fox trot?
No, but I once saw a goose step.

What do geese eat?
Gooseberries.

How are a goose and an old car alike?
They both honk.

What do cold geese suffer from?
Goose pimples.

Why are there fowls in football?
Because there are ducks in cricket.

What do you get if you cross a goose with an elephant?
An animal that honks before it runs you over.

Why do a flock of geese follow the leader?
He's got the map.

What is a good way to get a wild duck?
Bring a tame one out, and annoy it.

What bird is useful in boxing matches?
A duck.

Why do ducks always look so sad?
When they preen their feathers, they get down in the mouth.

What grows up while it grows down?
A baby duckling.

What is a crazy duck?
A wacky quacky.

What is a sick duck?
A mallardy.

What is a fast duck?
A quick quack.

What is a witty duck?
A wise-quack.

What would you get if you crossed a duck with an elephant?
Enough feathers to fill a duvet.

What would you get if you crossed a duck with a cow?
Milk and quackers.

What kind of doctor treats ducks?
A quack-doctor.

What happens to ducks when they fly upside down?
They quack up.

What has webbed feet and fangs?
Count Quacula.

What makes Donald Duck fall over?
Disney spells.

Why did Walt Disney give Donald Duck the sack?
Because he wasn't all he was quacked up to be.

What would you get if you crossed a drake with a big whale?
Moby Duck.

How do ducks dance?
Slow, slow, quack, quack, slow.

What is a duck's favourite dance?
The quackstep.

How did ducks get their flat feet?
Trying to teach elephants to dance.

What is a duck's favourite TV programme?
A duckumentary.

What else?
The feather forecast.

How do you get down from an elephant?
You don't, you get it from ducks.

What's the difference between a ballerina and a duck?
One dances in Swan Lake, the other swims in it.

What is a hot and noisy duck?
A firequacker.

What kind of duck robs banks?
A safe-quacker.

What do duck decorators do?
Paper over the quacks.

What has four legs, a yellow beak, and barks?
A ducks-hund.

What says 'quick, quick, quick'?
A duck with hiccups.

What do you call a scruffy cat that has just eaten a duck?
A duck-filled tattypuss.

What is full of words and quacks?
A duck-tionary.

'My dad raises ducks.'
'So what? Mine raises hell!'

Why do ducks have webbed feet?
To stamp out forest fires.

What's 'quack, quack'?
Double ducks.

What do you call a spirit that haunts farmyards?
A poultrygeist

What pantomime do ducks and chickens like best?
Mother Goose, of course.

Birds Of A Feather Jokes

What do birds say on Halloween?
'Twick or Tweet.'

What is a bird's favourite pop record?
'The Birdie Song.'

What's the difference between a bird and a fly?
A bird can fly, but a fly can't bird.

Why do birds in nests never argue?
Because they don't want to fall out.

Why are birds not wealthy?
Because money doesn't grow on trees.

What bird never tells the truth?
The lyre-bird.

What pies can fly?
Magpies.

What bird would you find on a coal-field?
The mynah.

What birds are religious?
Birds of prey.

What birds are always unhappy?
Bluebirds.

What is the fastest bird?
The swift.

What kind of birds do you usually find in captivity?
Jail-birds.

What bird can lift the heaviest weights?
A crane.

What bird is always with you when you eat?
A swallow.

What bird is always out of breath?
A puffin.

What bird likes stealing?
Robin.

What do you call a bird that's unwell?
Illegal.

What do you give a sick bird?
Tweetment.

How do birds stop themselves in the air?
With airbrakes.

What's the difference between a bird with one wing, and a bird with two wings?
There's a difference of a pinion.

Where do birds fly for their holidays?
The Canary Islands.

Why do birds fly south for the winter?
It's too far to walk.

Did you hear about the cat who took first prize in the bird show?
He ate the prize canary.

**What would you get if you crossed a canary
with an elephant?**
*I don't know, but when it sang it would make a
terrible noise!*

Why are elephants grey?
So you can tell them apart from canaries.

**What would you get if you crossed a canary
with a lion?**
*I don't know, but if it sang, you'd better
listen!*

**What would you get if you crossed a canary
with a lawn-mower?**
Shredded tweet.

**What would you get if you crossed a canary
with an alley cat?**
A cheeping tom.

**What weighs 1000kg, has 4 legs, flies and is
yellow?**
Two 500kg canaries.

What's yellow and succeeds?
A toothless canary.

What do you call a bird with a big snarl?
A budgerigrrrrrrr!

'Doctor, doctor, I keep thinking I'm a budgie.'
'Well, perch over there, and I'll tweet you in a minute.'

What can a budgie do, that we can't?
Take a bath in a saucer.

What would you get if you crossed a budgie with an elephant?
A VERY messy cage.

Why is an elephant like a budgie?
Neither can ride a bicycle.

What would you get if you crossed a budgie with a mummy?
A flying bandage.

What do you give a budgie for breakfast?
Tweetabix.

What do you do if you lose your budgie?
Contact the Flying Squad.

What's blue, and has a wing-span of 60 feet?
A 3-ton budgie.

What would you get if you crossed a parrot
with a lion?
*I don't know, but if it wanted a cracker, you'd
better give it one!*

What would you get if you crossed a parrot
with a seagull?
*A bird that makes a mess on your head, and
then says 'sorry'!*

What would you get if you crossed a parrot
with a watch?
Politics.

What would you get if you crossed a parrot
with an elephant?
Something that tells everything it remembers.

What would you get if you crossed a parrot
with a yak?
Yakety-yak!

What would you get if you crossed a parrot
with a homing pigeon?
A bird that asks its way if it gets lost.

What would you get if you crossed a parrot
with a canary?
*A bird that knows both the words and the
music.*

What would you get if you crossed a parrot
with a centipede?
A walkie-talkie.

What would you get if you crossed a parrot
with a crocodile?
*Something that will bite your head off, and say
'Who's a pretty boy, then?'*

What would you get if you crossed a parrot
with a woodpecker?
A bird that talks to you in Morse Code.

Who had a parrot that squawked 'pieces of
four?'
Short John Silver.

What's red and green and jumps out of
aeroplanes?
A parrot-trooper.

What do you call a single parrot?
Monopoly.

Where do parrots study?
A pollytechnic.

What do parrots eat?
Pollyfilla.

What's a polygon?
An empty parrot cage.

What do you call a Scottish parrot?
A Macaw.

Why did the parrot wear a raincoat?
It wanted to be polyunsaturated.

Why couldn't the parrot talk to the dove?
He didn't know pigeon English.

What would you get if you crossed a carrier pigeon with a woodpecker?
A bird that knocks before delivering its message.

What would you get if you crossed a pigeon with a zero?
A flying none.

What would you get if you crossed a pigeon with an elephant?
Dirty bus queues!

Why did the pigeon fly over the race-course?
It wanted to have a flutter on the horses.

What did one pigeon say to the other as they flew over the railway station?
'Let's do some train-spotting.'

What did one pigeon say to the other as they flew over a garage?
'Let's put a deposit on a Porsche.'

What do you call a woodpecker without a beak?
A head-banger.

Have you heard the joke about the woodpecker?
It's boring!

Why did the owl owl?
Because the woodpecker woodpecker.

What sits on a tree singing 'Hoots mon, hoots
mon?'
A Scottish owl.

If an elephant always remembers, what animal
always forgets?
An owl — it's always saying 'Who? who?'.

What would you get if you crossed an owl with
a goat?
A hootenanny.

What would you get if you crossed an owl with an oyster?
A bird that drops pearls of wisdom.

What would you get if you crossed an owl with a skunk?
A bird that smells, but doesn't give a hoot.

Why are owls wiser than chickens?
Have you ever heard of Kentucky Fried Owl?

What do lovesick owls say to each other when it's raining?
'To-wet-to-woo.'

What book tells you about famous owls?
'Who's Whoooo', of course.

Why does the owl make everyone laugh?
Because it's such a hoot.

Two black birds were sitting on a branch when one turned to the other and said: 'Bred any good rooks lately?'

Where do giant condors come from?
Eggs.

What would you get if you crossed a black bird
with a mad dog?
A raven maniac.

What do you give a constipated sparrow?
Chirrup of figs.

How would a wounded sparrow land safely?
By sparrowchute.

What's got six legs and can fly long distances?
Three swallows.

What would you get if you crossed a swallow
with an elephant?
Lots of broken telegraph poles.

What would you get if you crossed Boy George
with a bird of prey?
Vulture Club.

What would you get if you crossed an eagle
with a skunk?
An animal that stinks to high heaven.

What kind of hawk has no wings?
A tomahawk.

What do you call a man with a seagull on his head?
Cliff.

What has two legs, a big beak and hops?
A pelicangaroo.

Why should we feel sorry for the pelican?
He always has a big bill facing him.

What's a pelican's favourite fish?
Anything that fits the bill.

Why did the pelican put his leg in his mouth when he ate out?
He wanted to foot the bill.

What would you get if you crossed a pelican with an electric eel?
A big electric bill.

What sort of story did the peacock tell?
A beautiful long tale.

Why do hummingbirds hum?
Because they don't know the words.

What would you get if you crossed a hummingbird with a doorbell?
A humdinger.

What's the difference between Stork and butter?
Butter can't stand on one leg.

Why does a stork lift one leg?
If it lifted the other, it would fall over.

What's red, white and black?
A sunburnt penguin.

What's black and white and goes round and round?
A penguin caught in a revolving door.

What else?
A penguin in a spin-dryer.

What's black and white and makes a dreadful noise?
A penguin playing the bagpipes.

What's black and white, black and white, and black and white?
A penguin rolling down a hill.

What else?
A penguin on a zebra crossing.

Why don't polar bears eat Penguins?
They can't get the wrappers off.

What would you get if you crossed a penguin with a lamb?
A sheepskin dinner jacket.

What's 3m tall, yellow, with purple feet, and sings like a nightingale?
Nothing.

Jokes for Egg Heads

Who wrote Great Eggs-pectations?
Charles Chickens.

What philosophy do egg-head chickens study?
Eggs-istentialism.

What is mind?
No matter.

What is matter?
Never mind.

Who wrote *Thoughts of a China Cat?*
Chairman Miaow.

Who was the cleverest pig?
Albert Ein-swine.

What kind of jokes did Einstein make?
Wise cracks.

What's the centre of gravity?
The letter V.

What is copper nitrate?
Overtime for policemen.

Where do egg-heads live?
Braintree.

What's the definition of brain food?
Noodle soup.

What is a chicken's favourite play?
Shakespeare's Omlet.

What Shakespearean character invented hockey?
Puck.

Who were the world's smallest lovers?
Gnomeo and Juliet.

Who was the poet of basketball?
Longfellow.

Which poet wrote 'To a Nightingale'?
Whoever he was, I bet he didn't get a reply!

What Russian deer was a famous composer?
Moosorgski.

How do they judge exams in Russia?
You get Marx out of ten.

What did the French chicken say when she hatched her first egg?
'What on oeuf is this?'

What do Frenchmen eat for breakfast?
Huit heures bix.

What's it called when two French push-chairs collide?
A crèche.

What monster was the President of France?
Charles de Ghoul.

What do egg-head chickens read?
An hen-cyclopedia.

What do you call an egg-head chicken?
A hen-tellectual.

What do you call someone with a dictionary in his jeans?
Smarty pants.

Why are elephants egg-heads?
They have lots of grey matter.

What is an egg-otist?
Someone suffering from 'I'-strain.

How can you eat an egg without breaking its shell?
Ask someone else to do it.

What nut has no shell?
A doughnut.

Who invented algebra?
A clever X-pert.

What's right and never long?
An angle.

What did Thomas Edison Elephant invent?
The electric peanut.

What invention allows you to see through walls?
A window.

What's full of knowledge, but knows nothing at all?
A book-case.

What question can you never say 'yes' to?
~~'Are you asleep?'~~ WANT

What asks no questions, but demands an answer?
The telephone.

What has gone forever, and you'll never get back?
Yesterday.

Where does Friday come before Tuesday?
In the dictionary.

What is the longest word in the dictionary?
Elastic — it stretches.

What can you break with only one word?
Silence.

What can you hear, but not see; and only speaks when it's spoken to?
An echo.

What is a bore?
Someone with nothing to say, who says it.

What belongs to you, but is used by others?
Your name.

Who was one of the strongest dictators?
Muscle-ini.

Which mouse was the Emperor of Rome?
Julius Cheeser.

Who was the trifle's favourite artist?
Botti-jelly.

What famous artist had an arresting personality?
Constable.

What's the end of everything?
The letter G.

Jokes for Addle-brains and Bird-brains

Why did the addle-brain put the chicken in a hot bath?
So she'd lay hard-boiled eggs.

Did you hear about the addle-brain who thought egg shampoo came from a hen sitting on your head?

Did you hear about the addle-brain who boiled an egg for 15 minutes, and it still wasn't soft!

Did you hear about the bird-brain who bought a packet of bird-seed? He wanted to grow some chickens.

Did you hear about the bird-brain who found a feather in his bed, and thought he had chicken pox?

Did you hear about the bird-brain who did bird impressions? He ate worms!

Where do addle-brains live?
Addlestone.

Why did the addle-brain cross the road?
He wanted to get to the middle.

What happened when the addle-brain had a brain transplant?
The brain rejected him.

What's the distance between an addle-brain's ears?
Next to nothing.

Did you hear about the addle-brain who lost his job as a lift-operator, because he couldn't learn the route?

Did you hear about the addle-brained terrorist who tried to blow up a bus? He burnt his lips on the exhaust pipe.

Did you hear about the addle-brain who watered his light bulbs?

Did you hear about the addle-brain who drove his car in reverse because he knew his Highway Code backwards?

Did you hear about the addle-brain who invented a new kind of tea-bag? It was water-proof.

Did you hear about the addle-brain who couldn't tell porridge from putty? His windows fell out.

Did you hear about the bird-brain who didn't change the water in the goldfish bowl because the fish hadn't drunk it yet.

Where would you find an addle-brained shop-lifter?
Squashed under the shop.

What did he call his pet elephant?
Rover.

What did the bird-brain call his pet zebra?
Spot.

Why did the bird-brain cut a hole in the top of
his umbrella?
To see when it was raining.

Why did the bird-brain put glue on the top of
his head?
To help things stick in his mind.

Why did the bird-brain floodlight his sundial?
So he could see the time at night.

Why did the bird-brain drive into the sea?
He'd been told to dip his headlights.

Did you hear about the bird-brain who went to
a mind-reader, and got his money back?

How do you keep a bird-brain happy for a
whole morning?
Write P.T.O. on both sides of a sheet of paper.

What happened when the bird-brain changed his mind?
His new one didn't work either.

Did you hear about the bird-brain who went to the dentist to have a wisdom tooth put in?

Did you hear about the bird-brain who mopped up his spilt tea with a sponge cake?

What do you call a flea that lives in a bird-brain's head?
A space invader.

What did the bird-brain do with the flea in his head?
He shot it.

Did you hear about the addle-brained Morris dancer? He fell off the bonnet.

Did you hear about the addle-brain who addressed his letter upside down? It was going to Australia.

How do you make an addle-brain laugh on Easter Sunday?
Tell him a joke on Good Friday.

What would you get if crossed an addle-brain with a gooseberry?
Gooseberry fool.

Why are Londoners addle-brained?
Because the population is so dense.

Why did the addle-brain bury his car battery?
Because it was dead.

Why did the addle-brain jump out of the window?
To try his new jump-suit.

Why did the addle-brain aim a cannon at the peas?
He'd been told to shell them.

What's bird-brained and works with flowers?
A blooming idiot.

What's French for idiot?
Lagoon.

What's bright red and bird-brained?
A blood clot.

What's the difference between an addle-brain and a Welsh rarebit?
One's easy to cheat, and the other's cheesy to eat.

What's the difference between an addle-brain and a monkey?
You can hold a conversation with a monkey.

How can you tell the addle-brain on an oil-rig?
He's the one feeding bread to the helicopters.

Egg-stinct Jokes

How did dinosaurs pass their exams?
With extinction.

Why did the dinosaur cross the road?
There weren't any chickens in those days.

What's extinct and worked in rodeos?
A bronco-saurus.

What do you do with a blue dinosaur?
Cheer him up.

What is 20m long, and jumps every hour?
A dinosaur with hiccups.

What would you get if you crossed a prehistoric monster with a person sleeping?
A dinosnore.

What would you get if you crossed a prehistoric monster with a lemon?
A dinosour.

What would you get if you crossed a dinosaur with a witch?
Tyrannosaurus hex.

What do you call extinct ship disasters?
Tyrannosaurus wrecks.

Who was the first prehistoric novelist?
Charlotte Brontesaurus.

Two dodos watched a sailing ship come to their remote island. 'Quick, we'd better hide,' said one. 'Why? They look friendly enough,' said the other. 'Yes, but we're supposed to be extinct!'

What do you call a dinosaur who's been dead
and buried for millions of years?
Pete.

What's the difference between a dinosaur and a
sandwich?
The sandwich doesn't weigh 5 tons.

What followed the dinosaur?
Its tail.

What was once the biggest moth in the world?
The mammoth.

Why did the mammoth cross the road?
It was a trunk road.

What would you get if you crossed a mammoth
with the Abominable Snowman?
A jumbo yeti.

What newspaper did the cavemen read?
The Prehistoric Times.

Where would you see a prehistoric cow?
In a moo-seum.

What came after the Ice Age and the Stone
Age?
The sausage!

Eggs-terrestial Jokes

What dish is out of this world?
A flying saucer.

What do you call an eggs-terrestial body in an omelette pan?
An Unidentified Frying Object.

What flies around the kitchen at 100mph and glows yellow?
An Unidentified flying Omelette.

What is the best way to see a flying saucer?
Trip up a waiter.

What did one flying saucer say to the other?
'Friend UFO?'

A man saw a flying saucer land in his garden.
A creature got out that had three eyes and two
noses and which walked on its elbows.
'Take me to your leader', it said.
'No way', the man replied. 'What you need is a
plastic surgeon.'

How do Martians make tea?
Out of flying saucers.

What's soft, sweet and white and comes from
Mars?
A Martian mallow.

What is eggs-terrestial, and leads a parade?
A Martian band.

What's brown, woolly, covered in chocolate, and
goes round the sun?
A Mars Baa.

What did the Martian say when he landed in a flower bed?
'Take me to your weeder.'

What did the Martian say to the petrol pump?
'Take your finger out of your ear and listen to me.'

What did the traffic light say to the Martian?
'Don't look now, I'm changing!'

What do you call a fat ET?
An extra-cholesterol, or EC.

What did ET's mum say to him when he finally got home?
'Where on earth have you been?'

Eggs-otic Jokes

What do you call an Arab dairy farmer?
A milk sheik.

What game do the Arabs like to play?
Hide and sheik.

What's crunchy and lives in the Middle East?
Sultan vinegar crisps.

What is beige, goes on rails and travels
through the desert?
A camel train.

How do you play Russian roulette in India?
*Play the flute with six cobras, and try not to get
the cobra that's deaf.*

What do you call a small Indian guitar?
A baby-sitar.

How do Iranians speak on the telephone?
Persian to Persian.

How do you use an Egyptian doorbell?
Toot-and-come-in.

What is the speed limit in Egypt?
50 Niles per hour.

What language do they speak in Cuba?
Cubic.

What is the coldest country in the world?
Chile.

How do you make a Mexican chilli?
Send him to the South Pole.

What's yellow, comes from Peru, and is
completely unknown?
Euston bear.

What do Zulus do with banana skins?
Throw them away, of course!

What would you get if you crossed an Hawaiian dancer with an Indian brave?
A Hula Whoop.

What do fish sing in the South Pacific?
'Salmon Chanted Evening.'

What are government workers called in Seville?
Seville servants.

What's purple and 4000 miles long?
The Grape Wall of China.

What is Chinese and deadly?
Chop Sueycide.

What is the cheapest way to get to Australia?
Be born there.

What is a German's favourite Chinese take-away?
Sweet and sourkraut.

What is the commonest illness in China?
Kung Flu.

What did the fourteenth century Chinese wear to keep out the cold?
Ming coats.

Eggs-cruciating Jokes

What's white on the outside, brown on the inside, and tells eggs-cruciating jokes?
A corny beef sandwich.

Who wrote eggs-cruciating jokes and never grew up?
Peter Pun.

What's a joiner's favourite TV programme?
Plankety Plank.

Who was the world's first underwater spy?
James Pond.

What do you call a Scottish cloakroom attendant?
Angus McCoatup.

What's defeat?
What we walk on.

What's the difference between an elephant with tusk-ache, and a rainstorm?
One roars with pain, and the other pours with rain.

What's the difference between a mouldy lettuce and a dismal story?
One's a bad salad, and the other's a sad ballad.

What did two horses want in the theatre?
A couple of stalls.

What's the difference between a bus driver and a cold?
One knows the stops, the other stops the nose.

What's the difference between an angry audience and a cow with a sore throat?
One boos madly, and the other moos badly.

Where are the Andes?
At the end of your armies!

What helps keep your teeth together?
Toothpaste.

What's got two legs and bursts into flames?
Flared trousers.

What do you get if you cross a cowboy with a stew?
Hopalong Casserole.

What's a tea-pot's favourite song?
'Home, home on the range'.

What did Columbus see on his right hand when
he discovered America?
Five fingers.

Did you hear about the lorry load of wigs
stolen on the M25? The police are combing the
area.

Did you hear about the lorry load of dirty
saucepans stolen on the M25? The police are
scouring the countryside.

What do you call a man in a cemetery who's
wearing two coats?
Max Bygraves.

Un-eggs-purgated,
Eggs-certificate Jokes

What's a sick joke?
Something that comes up in conversation.

Knock, knock.
Who's there?
Nicholas.
Nicholas who?
Nicholas girls shouldn't climb trees.

Which rude saint is Santa Claus named after?
Saint Knickerless.

What is streaky bacon?
A pig running round with no clothes on.

What's the difference between a Peeping Tom
and someone who's just got out of the bath?
*One is rude and nosy, and the other is nude
and rosy.*

What goes 70mph on a washing-line?
Honda pants.

Why did the lobster turn red?
Because the sea weed.

What is black and comes out of the sea
shouting 'Knickers'?
Crude oil.

What is black and comes out of the sea
whispering 'Panties'?
Refined oil.

Who's short, scared of wolves, and swears?
Little Rude Riding Hood.

What happens if you walk under a cow?
You could get a pat on the head.

What's big, green and smells?
A monster's bottom.

What's round, red and rude?
Tomato sauce.

What do you call a rude cabbage?
A fresh vegetable.

How do you start a rude pudding race?
Sago to hell.

What's brown and sounds like a bell?
Dung!

Where do Londoners with spots live?
'Ackney.

Why did the secretary cut her fingers off?
She wanted to write shorthand.

'Mum, I wish we could have a dustbin like
other families.'
'Shut up, and keep eating.'

'Mum, why is Dad running so fast?'
'Shut up and reload the gun.'

How do you make a Venetian blind?
Stick your finger in his eye.

What's another name for a coffin?
A snuff-box.

What's green and swings through trees?
A septic monkey.

What is the soft stuff between a shark's teeth?
Slow swimmers.

What is long, horny, black, and smells of
cheese?
Your toenails.

Why are sausages so bad-mannered?
They spit in the frying-pan.

What do you call a woman with two toilets on
her head?
Lulu.

How does an elephant overtake a tortoise?
He steps on it.

Did you hear about the man who got a job at
the Zoo cleaning out the elephant house? Now
he's complaining that his work is piling up . . .